the GLUTEN-FREE
recipe book

the GLUTEN-FREE
recipe book

Bounty
BOOKS

The Gluten-Free Recipe Book

Publisher: Samantha Warrington
Managing Editor: Karen Rigden
Production Controller: Allison Gonsalves
Editor: Jane Birch
Designer: Chris Bell/cbdesign

Published in 2015 by Bounty Books,
a division of Octopus Publishing Group Ltd
Carmelite House
50 Victoria Embankment
London, EC4Y 0DZ
www.octopusbooks.co.uk

An Hachette UK Company
www.hachette.co.uk

ISBN: 978-0-753729-27-4

Printed and bound in China

contents

introduction 6

breakfasts 12

snacks & light meals 28

family favourites 52

food for friends 70

cakes & bakes 88

delicious desserts 108

index 126

acknowledgements 128

introduction

What is gluten?

Gluten is a type of protein found in a number of grains, including wheat, barley and rye. Gluten becomes sticky and malleable when combined with water, making it ideal for bread-making and baking.

What is coeliac disease?

Coeliac disease can develop at any age, but it is most commonly diagnosed in people aged between 40 and 50. When people with coeliac disease eat gluten-containing foods, their immune system fights the gluten, causing inflammation of the delicate cells lining the small intestine. In the process, the small intestine's villi – finger-like projections necessary for the absorption of nutrients and fluids from food and drink – become flattened and cannot do their job properly, causing digestive and nutritional upsets.

In recent years many people who do not suffer from coeliac disease have opted for a gluten-free or partially gluten-free diet because of the perceived health benefits, although there is no evidence to suggest that eliminating gluten from your diet has any health benefits if you are not gluten intolerant.

Following a gluten-free diet

When switching to a gluten-free diet, it may initially seem that there is nothing you can safely eat. A gluten-free diet rules out all ordinary baked goods, pasta and many convenience foods such as gravies, soups and sauces. This is because gluten is used as an additive in a wide number of foods including, for example, in ice cream and ketchup.

Careful thought needs to be given to shopping for and preparing gluten-free meals but there are many wonderful foods that are naturally gluten-free and you can use these to make delicious meals.

As with all diets, being organized is the best approach to ensure you eat well. Planning meals in advance, shopping with a list of foods you are allowed, reading food labels and cooking meals from scratch will all help to make life easier and ensure a balanced, varied and satisfying diet.

Gluten fact
Estimates suggest that up to 1 per cent of the population cannot tolerate gluten.

Foods that are naturally gluten-free

There are number of ingredients that can form the basis of a gluten-free diet that is full of flavour and variety. These include:

- Fruit and vegetables
- Unprocessed meat, poultry and fish, including shellfish
- Unprocessed cheeses, butter, milk, cream and natural yogurt
- Eggs
- Tofu
- Cooking oils
- Sugar, bicarbonate of soda, cream of tartar and yeast
- Plain nuts, seeds and pulses
- Rice and its products, including rice flour and rice noodles
- Gluten-free grains and their products such as buckwheat noodles and flour and polenta
- Vinegars, herbs and spices

Hidden ingredients

It is important to get into the habit of always checking the label for hidden gluten. The following ingredients may contain gluten:

- Barley
- Bran
- Breadcrumbs
- Bulgar or cracked wheat
- Cereal extract, cereal binder
- Cracker meal
- Durum
- Farro
- Farina
- Kamut
- Modified starch
- Rusk
- Semolina
- Spelt
- Vegetable gum, vegetable protein, vegetable starch
- Wheat bran, wheatgerm, wheat starch
- Wheat, wholewheat

Storecupboard essentials

In addition to all the foods mentioned on the previous page, if you look out for and stock up on these specialist ingredients, you can make a wide range of mouthwatering gluten-free recipes.

Flours There are gluten-free flours that can be used for baking and cooking, such as rice, chickpea, corn, soya, buckwheat and millet. If your local supermarket doesn't stock them, you can find them at health-food stores or online.

Xanthan gum This powder is a huge help in gluten-free baking as it replaces, to some extent, the elastic qualities that gluten-free flours lack. Adding it to these flours makes bread less crumbly and pastry easier to roll and handle. You'll find in some supermarkets, online and in health-food stores.

Gluten-free baking powder Standard baking powder contains gluten so you'll need gluten-free for baking. It is now widely available in the baking aisle of supermarkets.

Pasta and noodles Gluten-free pasta is becoming more common and you'll find it in most supermarkets. Rice noodles and the varieties of soba noodles made entirely from buckwheat are naturally gluten-free.

Eating out
Check the menu carefully for hidden gluten, especially in sauces and coatings (such as breadcrumbs). Many chefs are happy to cook something off-menu to suit you.

Can I eat oats?
Most people with coeliac disease can eat gluten-free oats. Many brands of oats are produced in the same place as wheat, barley and rye, which makes them unsafe, so check that they guaranteed gluten-free.

quinoa

Grains Quinoa is a great addition to any diet, providing an excellent source of protein in addition to being gluten-free. It is a good substitute for couscous or bulgar wheat in salads and side dishes. Polenta is good for baking and can be used as an alternative to breadcrumbs for coating.

Cheese and dairy products Unprocessed cheeses are gluten-free, as is milk and plain, unflavoured yogurt, so these are worth keeping on hand.

Beware contamination

As well as avoiding all the obvious sources, it is important to ensure that your gluten-free foods are not cross-contaminated by others that contain gluten. For example, shop-bought meringues are likely to have come into contact with gluten-containing cakes, while chips from a fish and chip shop may have met with batter in the deep-fat fryer. Make these simple steps part of your daily routine:

* Store gluten-free flours separately
* Use separate spoons, knives and chopping boards to prepare gluten-free food
* Keep separate equipment, such as rolling pins, pastry brushes and sieves, for gluten-free baking
* Wash everything well and clean surfaces before cooking
* Never share breadboards, toasters or butter dishes with users of standard bread.

Gluten-free foods at a glance

Food type	Foods allowed	Foods to avoid/check
Cereals/grains	Maize, all types of rice, sorghum, sago, millet, tapioca, buckwheat, teff, quinoa, rice bran, oats, oat bran	Wheat, barley, rye, spelt, triticale, kamut, bulgar wheat, couscous, durum wheat, semolina, wheat bran
Flours	Rice, corn, soya, potato, chestnut, maize, gram, sorghum, tapioca, oat flour	All types of wheat, rye flour
Breakfast cereals	Any made from permitted cereals	Any made using wheat, rye, barley
Baked foods, pasta	Gluten-free breads, biscuits, crispbreads, cakes, pastries, biscuits, rusks, pastries, flour mix, pasta	Conventional breads, cakes, crispbreads, pasta, ice-cream cones
Meat, poultry, fish and eggs	All plain-cooked varieties and when used in dishes/products with gluten-free ingredients	Savoury pies, pasties, sausages, crumbed, battered, stuffed and processed products
Milk and milk products	Milk, most yogurts, cream, most cheeses; soya milks, yogurts and cheeses; tofu	Yogurt with crunchy ingredients; soya; some artificial creams and processed cheeses
Fats	Butter, margarine, oils, lard, dripping	Suet, some brands of low-fat spread
Vegetables	All types: fresh, frozen, dried, juiced (check ingredients if canned or in ready-made salads or bean and vegetable dishes)	Vegetables in sauce or dressing made using wheat flour; crumbed or battered vegetables; potato waffles and croquettes
Fruit	All types: fresh, frozen, dried, juiced, canned	Some fruit-pie fillings
Soups, sauces	All types thickened/made with gluten-free ingredients; some canned and dried soups	Gravy mixes, soups and sauces made with non-permitted flour or pasta
Snack foods	Plain nuts and seeds, some brands of crisps, savoury snacks, dips, sweets and chocolates	Sweet and savoury snacks made using non-permitted flours, liquorice
Drinks	Wine, spirits, liqueurs, cider; tea, pure coffee, cocoa, fizzy drinks, juices, most squashes and soft drinks	Real ales, beer, lager, stout; coffee or other drinks containing barley, malted drinks, vending-machine drinks
Miscellaneous	Pure salt, pepper, herbs, spices, vinegar, bicarbonate of soda, cream of tartar; curry powder, baking powder, yeast, essences, dressings, honey, jams, molasses, marmalade, nut butters	Spices, baking powders, dressings or any other ingredients containing wheat, rye or barley; some medicines and vitamins; spreads containing wheat flour

breakfasts

porridge with prune compote

serves 4–8
prep + cook time 25 minutes + cooling time

1 litre (1¾ pints) skimmed or
   semi-skimmed milk
500 ml (17 fl oz) water
1 teaspoon vanilla extract
pinch of ground cinnamon
pinch of salt
200 g (7 oz) porridge oats
3 tablespoons flaked almonds,
   toasted

compote
250 g (8 oz) ready-to-eat dried
   Agen prunes
125 ml (4 fl oz) apple juice
1 small cinnamon stick
1 clove
1 tablespoon mild agave nectar
   or runny honey
1 unpeeled orange quarter

1 Place all the compote ingredients in a small saucepan over a medium heat. Simmer gently for 10–12 minutes or until softened and slightly sticky. Leave to cool. (The compote can be prepared in advance and chilled.)
2 Put the milk, measurement water, vanilla extract, cinnamon and salt in a large saucepan over a medium heat and bring slowly to the boil. Stir in the oats, then reduce the heat and simmer gently, stirring occasionally, for 8–10 minutes until creamy and tender.
3 Spoon the porridge into bowls, scatter with the almonds and serve with the prune compote.

Tip
Perfect for a winter morning, this porridge contains oats, which are rich in magnesium which helps to prevent heart disease and is key to energy production.

breakfast cereal bars

makes 16
prep + cook time 45 minutes

100 g (3½ oz) butter, softened, plus
    extra for greasing
25 g (1 oz) soft light brown sugar
2 tablespoons golden syrup
125 g (4 oz) millet flakes
50 g (2 oz) quinoa
50 g (2 oz) dried cherries or
    cranberries
75 g (3 oz) sultanas
25 g (1 oz) sunflower seeds
25 g (1 oz) sesame seeds
25 g (1 oz) linseeds
40 g (1½ oz) unsweetened
    desiccated coconut
2 eggs, lightly beaten

1 Grease a 28 x 20 cm (11 x 8 inch) shallow baking tin.
2 Beat together the butter, sugar and syrup in a large bowl until creamy. Add all the remaining ingredients and beat well until combined.
3 Spoon the mixture into the prepared tin, level the surface with the back of a dessertspoon and place in a preheated oven, 180°C (350°F), Gas Mark 4, for 35 minutes until deep golden. Remove from the oven and leave to cool in the tin.
4 Turn out on to a wooden board and carefully cut into 16 fingers using a serrated knife. Store in an airtight container for up to 5 days.

fruity summer smoothie

makes 4 x 300 ml (½ pint) glasses
prep time 5 minutes

2 peaches, halved, pitted and
    chopped
300 g (10 oz) strawberries
300 g (10 oz) raspberries
400 ml (14 fl oz) skimmed or
    semi-skimmed milk
ice cubes

1 Put the peaches in a blender or food processor with the strawberries and raspberries and blend to a smooth purée, scraping the mixture down from the sides of the bowl if necessary.
2 Add the milk and blend the ingredients again until the mixture is smooth and frothy. Pour the smoothie over the ice cubes in tall glasses.

Tip
A fruit-packed smoothie is great for breakfast on the go – filling and nutritious, it also counts towards your five fruit and veg a day.

crunchy honey yogurt

serves 6
prep + cook time 15 minutes + cooling time

500 g (1 lb) Greek yogurt
125 g (4 oz) strawberries, quartered

topping
50 g (2 oz) flaked almonds
50 g (2 oz) pumpkin seeds
50 g (2 oz) sunflower seeds
3 tablespoons sesame seeds
50 g (2 oz) oats
6 tablespoons golden caster sugar
4 tablespoons clear honey, plus extra to drizzle (optional)

1 Mix the almonds, seeds, oats and sugar in a large bowl. Line a large baking sheet with nonstick baking paper, then pour the nut and seed mixture over. Lightly shake the baking sheet to level the ingredients.

2 Drizzle the honey in thin streams over the top, then place under a preheated medium grill for 3–4 minutes until the sugar begins to caramelize and the nuts and seeds turn golden brown. Remove from the grill and set aside to cool and harden. Place the hardened nuts and seeds in a polythene bag and bash with a rolling pin to crush into a crunchy topping.

3 Spoon the yogurt into a bowl and fold in the strawberries. Divide among 6 serving bowls and sprinkle with the topping. (Store any leftover topping in an airtight container for up to 2 weeks.) Drizzle with more honey, if liked.

Tip
With seeds and nuts for essential fats, calcium-rich yogurt and strawberries for vitamins, minerals and antioxidants, breakfast doesn't get much better for you that this.

muesli

serves 4
prep time 10 minutes

200 g (7 oz) rolled oats
50 g 2 oz) dried cranberries
50 g (2 oz) dried apricots, chopped
50 g (2 oz) dates, chopped
50 g (2 oz) pecan nuts, chopped
50 g (2 oz) Brazil nuts, chopped
3–4 tablespoons seeds, such as
   sunflower, pumpkin and sesame

to serve
milk
natural yogurt
fresh fruit

1 Mix together all the dry ingredients.
2 Divide among 4 bowls and serve with milk, yogurt and fresh fruit.

herby smoked salmon omelettes

serves 4
prep + cook time 25 minutes

8 large eggs
2 spring onions, thinly sliced
2 tablespoons chopped chives
2 tablespoons chopped chervil
50 g (2 oz) butter
4 thin slices of smoked salmon,
   cut into thin strips, or 125 g
   (4 oz) smoked salmon trimmings
pepper

1 Put the eggs, spring onions and herbs in a bowl, beat together lightly and season with pepper.
2 Heat a medium-sized frying pan over a medium-low heat, add a quarter of the butter and melt until beginning to froth. Pour in a quarter of the egg mixture and swirl to cover the base of the pan. Stir gently for 2–3 minutes or until almost set.
3 Sprinkle over a quarter of the smoked salmon strips and cook for a further 30 seconds or until just set. Fold over and slide on to a serving plate. Repeat to make 3 more omelettes. Serve omelettes immediately.

Tip
This dish also makes a delicious brain-boosting lunch, accompanied by a baby leaf and herb salad and perhaps some steamed new potatoes.

melting mushrooms

serves 4
prep + cook time 25 minutes

2 tablespoon olive oil
4 large flat mushrooms
4 small fresh tomatoes, roughly
   chopped
1 tablespoon tomato purée
4 tablespoons canned cannellini
   beans, drained and rinsed
1 tablespoon clear honey
1 tablespoon chopped parsley
50 g (2 oz) Gruyère or Edam
   cheese, thinly sliced
1 tablespoon freshly grated
   Parmesan cheese
4 slices gluten-free wholemeal
   toast, to serve

1 Heat the oil in a large, heavy-based frying pan and cook the mushrooms over a moderate heat for 2–3 minutes, turning once, until they are softened. Place the mushrooms, stalk side up, on a foil-lined grill rack.

2 Add the tomatoes to the pan juices, and cook, stirring occasionally, for 4–5 minutes until the tomatoes are thick and pulpy. Add the tomato purée, beans and honey and continue to cook for a further 1 minute. Remove from the heat and stir in the parsley.

3 Divide the mixture between the mushrooms and arrange the slices of Gruyère or Edam over the top. Sprinkle the mushrooms with the Parmesan and place under a preheated hot grill for 2–3 minutes until golden and bubbling. Serve with slices of hot buttered wholemeal toast.

bacon & egg crispy bread tarts

serves 4
prep + cook time 45 minutes

spray olive oil, for oiling
16 slices of gluten-free white bread
75 g (3 oz) butter, melted
150 g (5 oz) smoked bacon
   rashers, rind removed, diced
2 eggs
125 ml (4 fl oz) double cream
2 tablespoons freshly grated
   Parmesan cheese
8 vine cherry tomatoes
salt and pepper

1 Spray a muffin tray lightly with spray oil. Cut the crusts off the bread and discard. Flatten each bread slice by rolling over it firmly with a rolling pin. Brush each slice with the melted butter and place 8 of the slices diagonally on top of the others to form the bases. Carefully press each base into a hole of the prepared muffin tray, making sure that they fit evenly (they need to reach up the sides).

2 Bake in a preheated oven, 200°C (400°F), Gas Mark 6, for 12–15 minutes until crisp and golden.

3 Meanwhile, heat a dry frying pan until hot, add the bacon and cook for 2–3 minutes until crisp and golden.

4 Divide the bacon among the baked bread cases. Beat together the eggs, cream, cheese and salt and pepper to taste in a bowl. Spoon into the cases and top each with a cherry tomato. Bake in the oven for 15 minutes until set.

ranch-style eggs

serves 4
prep + cook time 30 minutes

2 tablespoons olive oil
1 onion, finely sliced
1 red chilli, deseeded and finely
    chopped
1 garlic clove, crushed
1 teaspoon ground cumin
1 teaspoon dried oregano
400 g (13 oz) canned cherry
    tomatoes
200 g (7 oz) roasted red and
    yellow peppers in oil (from a jar),
    drained and roughly chopped
4 eggs
salt and pepper
4 tablespoons finely chopped
    coriander, to garnish

1 Heat the oil in a large frying pan and add the onion, chilli, garlic, cumin and oregano.
2 Fry gently for about 5 minutes or until soft then add the tomatoes and peppers and cook for a further 5 minutes. If the sauce looks dry, add a splash of water.
3 Season well and make 4 hollows in the mixture, break an egg into each and cover the pan. Cook for 5 minutes or until the eggs are just set.
4 Serve immediately, garnished with chopped coriander.

Tip
Eggs are an excellent source of low-fat protein. One egg has only about 80 calories and packs 6.5 grams of protein.

potato drop scones

serves 4
prep + cook time 30 minutes

550 g (1 lb 2 oz) large potatoes,
    peeled and cut into small
    chunks
1½ teaspoons gluten-free baking
    powder
2 eggs
75 ml (3 fl oz) milk
vegetable oil, for frying
salt and pepper

1 Cook the potatoes in a saucepan of salted boiling water for
15 minutes or until tender. Drain well, return to the pan and mash until
smooth. Leave to cool slightly.
2 Beat in the baking powder, then the eggs, milk and a little
seasoning, and continue to beat until everything is evenly combined.
3 Heat a little oil in a heavy-based frying pan. Drop heaped
dessertspoonfuls of the mixture into the pan, spacing them slightly
apart, and fry for 3–4 minutes, turning once, until golden. Transfer to
a serving plate and keep warm while frying the remainder of the potato
mixture.
4 Serve warm, instead of toast, with your favourite cooked breakfast.

**For salmon
potato drop scones**
add 100 g (3½ oz)
chopped smoked salmon,
2 tablespoons snipped
chives and 3 sliced
spring onions to the
potato mixture and
cook as above.

blueberry pancakes

serves 4
prep + cook time 20 minutes

125 g (4 oz) self-raising gluten-free
　flour
1 teaspoon gluten-free baking
　powder
1 egg
150 ml (¼ pint) soya milk
25 g (1 oz) unsalted butter, melted
100 g (3½ oz) blueberries
1 tablespoon olive oil

to serve
crème fraîche
maple syrup

1 In a large bowl whisk together the flour and baking powder.
2 Whisk together the egg and milk and whisk into the flour until smooth
3 Whisk in the melted butter, then stir in 75 g (3 oz) of the blueberries
4 Heat the oil in a frying pan over a medium heat, then spoon tablespoons of the mixture into the pan. Cook for 3–4 minutes until golden underneath, then flip over and cook for a further 2–3 minutes. Repeat with the remaining batter.
5 Serve with the remaining blueberries, a dollop of crème fraîche and a drizzle of maple syrup.

snacks &
light meals

bean & parsley pâté

serves 4
prep time 10 minutes

2 x 400 g (13 oz) cans beans,
  such as haricot or cannellini
  beans, rinsed and drained
3 tablespoons sun-dried tomato
  paste
2 teaspoons lemon juice
½ teaspoon ground cumin
  (optional)
4 tablespoons natural or Greek
  yogurt
2 tablespoons chopped parsley,
  plus extra to garnish
salt and pepper
hot gluten-free toast, to serve

1 Place the beans in a food processor with the sun-dried tomato paste, lemon juice and ground cumin, if using. Pulse to a thick, rough-textured paste, then add just enough of the yogurt to create a spreadable pâté.
2 Scrape the pâté into a bowl, stir in the parsley, then season to taste and serve with plenty of hot toast, garnished with extra parsley.

Tip
You can vary
the white beans you
use in this versatile
recipe – butterbeans
work well – and you
can swap the parsley
for fresh coriander
leaves or basil
too.

crostini with pea & ricotta pesto

serves 6
prep + cook time 20 minutes + cooling

1 small gluten-free French stick, sliced
3 tablespoons extra virgin olive oil, plus extra to serve
250 g (8 oz) fresh or frozen shelled peas
1 small garlic clove, crushed
50 g (2 oz) ricotta cheese
juice of ½ lemon
1 tablespoon chopped mint
15 g (½ oz) Parmesan cheese, freshly grated
salt and pepper

1 Lay the bread slices on a baking sheet, brush lightly with 1 tablespoon of the oil and bake in a preheated oven, 190°C (375°F), Gas Mark 5, for 5–6 minutes until crisp and golden. Leave to cool on a wire rack while you prepare the pesto.

2 Cook the peas in a saucepan of lightly salted boiling water for 3 minutes. Drain and immediately refresh under cold water. Put the peas in a food processor, add the remaining oil, the garlic, ricotta, lemon juice, mint, Parmesan and salt and pepper and process until fairly smooth.

3 Spread the crostini with the pesto and serve drizzled with oil.

cream of leek & pea soup

serves 6
prep + cook time 35 minutes

2 tablespoons olive oil
375 g (12 oz) leeks, slit and well
   washed then thinly sliced
375 g (12 oz) fresh shelled or
   frozen peas
small bunch mint
900 ml (1½ pints) vegetable or
   chicken stock
150 g (5 oz) mascarpone cheese
grated rind of 1 small lemon
salt and pepper

to garnish
mint leaves (optional)
lemon rind curls (optional)

1 Heat the oil in a saucepan, add the leeks, toss in the oil then cover and fry gently for 10 minutes, stirring occasionally, until softened but not coloured. Mix in the peas and cook briefly.
2 Pour the stock into the pan, add a little salt and pepper then bring to the boil. Cover and simmer gently for 10 minutes.
3 Ladle half the soup into a blender or food processor, add all the mint and blend until smooth. Pour the purée back into the saucepan. Mix the mascarpone with half of the lemon rind, reserving the rest for a garnish. Spoon half the mixture into the soup, then reheat, stirring until the mascarpone has melted. Taste and adjust the seasoning if needed. Ladle the soup into bowls, top with spoonfuls of the remaining mascarpone and a sprinkling of the remaining lemon rind. Garnish with mint leaves and lemon rind curls, if liked.

spiced vegetable & chickpea soup

serves 4
prep + cook time 20 minutes

2 tablespoons olive or vegetable
   oil
1 onion, chopped
1 green or red pepper, chopped
1 aubergine, diced
2 teaspoons peeled and chopped
   fresh root ginger
1 teaspoon chilli flakes
6 tomatoes, roughly diced
900 ml (1½ pints) hot vegetable
   stock
400 g (13 oz) can chickpeas,
   rinsed and drained
salt and pepper

1 Heat the oil in a large saucepan and cook the vegetables and ginger for 7–8 minutes until slightly softened. Add the chilli flakes, tomatoes, hot stock and chickpeas and bring to the boil. Reduce the heat and simmer gently for about 10 minutes until the vegetables are tender.

2 Use a hand-held blender to blend until smooth. Season to taste, then ladle into mugs to serve.

Tip
Nutty and delicious, chickpeas are super-rich in iron, vitamins and minerals for an all-round health boost. Try them in salads, soups, curries and stews.

split pea & parsnip soup

serves 6
prep + cook time 1 hour 30 minutes
+ soaking time

250 g (8 oz) yellow split peas,
    soaked overnight in cold water
300 g (10 oz) parsnips, cut into
    chunks
1 onion, roughly chopped
1.5 litres (2½ pints) chicken or
    vegetable stock
salt and pepper

coriander butter
1 teaspoon cumin seeds, roughly
    crushed
1 teaspoon coriander seeds,
    roughly crushed
2 garlic cloves, finely chopped
75 g (3 oz) butter
small bunch of coriander

1 Drain the soaked split peas and put them into a saucepan with the parsnips, onion and stock. Bring to the boil and boil for 10 minutes. Reduce the heat, cover and simmer for 1 hour or until the split peas are soft.

2 Meanwhile, make the butter by dry-frying the cumin and coriander seeds and garlic in a small saucepan until lightly toasted. Mix into the butter with the coriander leaves and a little salt and pepper. Shape into a sausage shape on clingfilm or foil, wrap up and chill until needed.

3 Roughly mash the soup or purée in batches in a blender or food processor, if preferred. Reheat and stir in half the coriander butter until melted. Add a little extra stock if needed then season to taste. Ladle into bowls and top each bowl with a slice of the coriander butter.

For chilli butter, as an alternative to coriander butter, mix 75 g (3 oz) butter with grated rind and juice of 1 lime, 2 chopped spring onions and half a finely chopped red chilli.

fig, raspberry & prosciutto salad

serves 4–6
prep time 5 minutes

150 g (5 oz) rocket and beetroot
   salad mix
6 ripe figs, halved
150 g (5 oz) raspberries
8 slices of prosciutto
2 large buffalo mozzarella balls,
   each about 150 g (5 oz)

dressing
2 tablespoons aged balsamic
   vinegar
2 tablespoons olive oil

1 Put the rocket and beetroot leaves in a large bowl, add the halved figs, the raspberries and the prosciutto, toss carefully and transfer to a large serving plate.
2 Make the dressing by whisking together the vinegar and oil. Tear each mozzarella ball into 3 pieces and arrange them on the salad. Drizzle the dressing over the salad and serve.

For prosciutto-wrapped figs, to serve as a simple summer starter, cut 4 ripe figs in half and wrap each in a slice of prosciutto.

prawn, pea shoot & quinoa salad

serves 4
prep + cook time 25 minutes + cooling time

300 g (10 oz) quinoa
75 g (3 oz) mangetout, blanched and halved
200 g (7 oz) asparagus spears, cooked, cooled and cut into bite-sized pieces
50 g (2 oz) pea shoots
400 g (13 oz) cooked tiger prawns, shells removed
salt and pepper

fruit & nut dressing
2 tablespoons olive oil
2 tablespoons lemon juice
20 g (¾ oz) dried cranberries
50 g (2 oz) hazelnuts, chopped and toasted

1 Cook the quinoa according to the instructions on the packet. Set aside to cool.
2 Stir the mangetout and asparagus through the quinoa.
3 Make the dressing by mixing together the oil, lemon juice, cranberries and hazelnuts.
4 Spoon the pea shoots and prawns over the quinoa, drizzle over the dressing and serve.

warm chicken liver, butternut squash & bacon salad

serves 4
prep + cook time 30 minutes

4 tablespoons olive oil
750 g (1½ lb) butternut squash,
   deseeded and cut into small
   chunks (peeled if liked)
380 g (12½ oz) chicken livers,
   thawed if frozen and drained
175 g (6 oz) streaky bacon, cut into
   strips
100 g (3½ oz) walnuts
160 g (5½ oz) watercress
pepper
balsamic vinegar, to serve

1 Heat 3 tablespoons of the oil in a large, heavy-based frying pan or wok and cook the butternut squash, stirring occasionally, over a moderately high heat for 15–20 minutes until softened and cooked through.

2 Meanwhile, in a separate heavy-based frying pan heat the remaining oil and cook the chicken livers and bacon, stirring almost continually to prevent sticking, over a high heat for 10 minutes or until golden and cooked through. Add the walnuts and cook for a further minute to warm through.

3 Toss together the chicken livers, bacon, walnuts and butternut squash in a large bowl, season with pepper and set aside to cool for 3–4 minutes.

4 Just before serving toss the watercress into the bowl. Arrange the salad on 4 serving plates and drizzle with balsamic vinegar.

Tip
Butternut squash is equally delicious served mashed or roasted and is packed with vitamin A: one cupful is enough to supply over 400 per cent of your daily needs.

mediterranean rice salad

serves 4
prep + cook time 15 minutes + cooling time

75 g (3 oz) broccoli, finely chopped
75 g (3 oz) courgettes, finely chopped
75 g (3 oz) mixed red and yellow peppers, finely chopped
25 g (1 oz) spring onions, finely chopped
40 g (1½ oz) mushrooms, finely sliced
2 tablespoons water
2 tablespoons pesto
50 g (2 oz) cooked brown rice
50 g (2 oz) cooked wild rice
salt and pepper
parmesan shavings, to serve

1 Heat a large frying pan or wok, add the vegetables and the measured water and cook over a high heat for 3–5 minutes, until the vegetables have softened. Remove from the heat and allow to cool.
2 Mix the cooled vegetables with the pesto and cooked rice, season well and stir to combine. Cover and chill until required. Serve topped with a few Parmesan shavings and some basil leaves, if liked.

wild rice & turkey salad

serves 4
prep + cook time 40 minutes + cooling time

300 g (10 oz) wild rice
2 green apples, finely sliced
75 g (3 oz) pecan nuts
rind and juice of 2 oranges
60 g (2¼ oz) cranberries
3 tablespoons olive oil
2 tablespoons chopped parsley
4 turkey fillets, each about 125 g
   (4 oz)
salt and pepper

1 Cook the rice according to the instructions on the packet and allow to cool to room temperature.
2 Mix the apples into the rice with the pecans, the orange rind and juice and the cranberries. Season to taste with salt and pepper.
3 Mix together the oil and parsley. Cut the turkey fillets into halves or thirds lengthways and cover with this mixture. Heat a frying pan until it is hot but not smoking and cook the turkey for 2 minutes on each side. Slice the turkey, arrange the pieces next to the rice salad and serve immediately.

Tip
Wild rice is actually the seeds of four species of North American and Chinese aquatic grasses and is completely different to other kinds of rice.

mixed mushroom, herb & chicken frittata

serves 4
prep + cook time 20 minutes

1 tablespoon olive oil
1 skinless chicken breast fillet,
    sliced
200 g (7 oz) mixed mushrooms,
    such as chestnut, oyster and
    shiitake, sliced
1 red pepper, cored, deseeded and
    chopped
4 spring onions, sliced
8 eggs
3 tablespoons chopped herbs,
    such as parsley, chives and
    thyme
125 g (4 oz) low-fat soft cheese
    with chives
salt and pepper

1 Heat the oil in a large, nonstick frying pan. Add the chicken, mushrooms, red pepper and spring onions and cook over a high heat, stirring, for 5 minutes or until the chicken is cooked and the vegetables are tender.

2 Beat the eggs with the herbs and season with salt and pepper. Pour into the pan over the chicken and vegetables and cook gently for about 5 minutes or until set around the edges.

3 Dot the soft cheese over the top of the frittata and place the pan under a medium grill. Cook until the frittata is just set and the top is golden. Serve warm or cold.

Tip
A frittata is easier to make than a quiche and, as it doesn't have pastry, it is better for you too. Served cold, it is ideal for picnics and lunchboxes.

spiced courgette fritters

serves 4
prep + cook time 25 minutes

100 g (3½ oz) gram flour
1 teaspoon gluten-free baking
    powder
½ teaspoon ground turmeric
2 teaspoons ground coriander
1 teaspoon ground cumin
1 teaspoon chilli powder
250 ml (8 fl oz) soda water, chilled
625 g (1¼ lb) courgettes, cut into
    thick batons
salt
sunflower oil, for deep frying
natural yogurt, to dip

1 Sift the gram flour, baking powder, turmeric, coriander, cumin and chilli powder into a large mixing bowl. Season with salt and gradually add the soda water to make a thick batter, being careful not to overmix.

2 Pour sunflower oil into a wok until one-third full and heat to 180–190°C (350–375°F), or until a cube of bread browns in 30 seconds. Dip the courgette batons in the spiced batter and then deep-fry in batches for 1–2 minutes or until crisp and golden. Remove with a slotted spoon and drain on kitchen paper. Serve the courgettes immediately with natural yogurt, to dip.

Tip
Gram flour has a strong, slightly nutty taste and is naturally gluten-free. Made from ground chickpeas, it is popular in Indian cooking.

salmon & sesame skewers

serves 4
prep + cook time 30 minutes

1 tablespoon gluten-free soy
    sauce
2 teaspoons honey
500g (1 lb) salmon fillet, skinned
    and cut into strips
4 teaspoons sesame oil
juice of 1 lime
1 cucumber
6 spring onions, finely sliced
16 cherry tomatoes, halved
3 tablespoons sesame seeds

1 Mix together the soy sauce and honey in a shallow bowl. Add the salmon and mix well, then cover and leave to marinate in the refrigerator for 12–15 minutes. Meanwhile, soak 8 wooden skewers in water for 10 minutes.

2 Mix together the sesame oil and lime juice in a large bowl. Using a vegetable peeler, slice the cucumber into long, thin strips and place in the bowl with the spring onions and cherry tomatoes. Toss in the dressing.

3 Thread the salmon on to the skewers, then roll in the sesame seeds to coat. Cook in a preheated hot griddle pan or under a preheated hot grill for 2–3 minutes on each side or until cooked through.

4 Serve the salmon skewers with the cucumber salad.

peppered chicken skewers

serves 4
prep + cook time 20 minutes + marinating time

4 boneless, skinless chicken
    breasts, about 150 g (5 oz) each
2 tablespoons finely chopped
    rosemary, plus extra to garnish
2 garlic cloves, finely chopped
3 tablespoons lemon juice
2 teaspoons mustard
1 tablespoon clear honey
2 teaspoons freshly ground black
    pepper
1 tablespoon olive oil
pinch of salt
lemon wedges, to serve

1 Lay a chicken breast between 2 sheets of clingfilm and flatten slightly with a rolling pin or meat mallet. Repeat with the remaining chicken breasts, then cut the chicken into thick strips.
2 Put the chicken strips in a non-metallic bowl and add the remaining ingredients. Mix well, then cover and leave to marinate in the refrigerator for 5–10 minutes. Meanwhile, soak 8 wooden skewers in water for 10 minutes.
3 Thread the chicken strips on to the skewers and cook under a preheated medium-hot grill for 4–5 minutes on each side or until the chicken is cooked through. Garnish with rosemary, and serve immediately with lemon wedges.

baked sweet potatoes with prawns

serves 4
prep + cook time 35 minutes

1 tablespoon olive oil
4 large sweet potatoes, skin on,
   scrubbed, patted dry
250 g (8 oz) medium prawns,
   defrosted if frozen
1 ripe avocado, peeled, stoned
   and cut into small chunks
2 tablespoons mayonnaise
2 tablespoons milk or water
3 tablespoons crème fraîche
1 tablespoon tomato purée

to serve
ground paprika
1 small pot sprouting alfalfa
   or other sprouting seeds

1 Drizzle a little of the oil over each sweet potato, then rub it all over the skin. Put the potatoes on a baking sheet. Bake in a preheated oven, 200°C (400°F), Gas Mark 6, for 25–30 minutes until tender and cooked through.

2 Meanwhile, place the prawns and avocado in a bowl and toss together. Mix the mayonnaise with the milk or water until smooth, then add the crème fraîche and tomato purée and mix until well blended. Add the prawns and avocado and toss well to coat lightly.

3 Remove the sweet potatoes from the oven. Split the hot potatoes and fill them with the prawn mixture. Serve garnished with a pinch of paprika and some freshly cut sprouting seeds.

deluxe eggs florentine

serves 4
prep + cook time 30 minutes

12 asparagus spears, trimmed
2 tablespoons butter, plus extra for
   buttering
150 g (5 oz) baby spinach
pinch of freshly grated nutmeg
2 English muffins, halved and
   lightly toasted
1 tablespoon vinegar
4 large eggs
8 tablespoons ready-made
   hollandaise sauce, to serve
salt and pepper

1 Blanch the asparagus spears in a pan of boiling water for 2–3 minutes, drain and keep warm.

2 Meanwhile, melt the butter in a large frying pan, add the spinach and stir-fry for 3 minutes or until just wilted. Season with grated nutmeg, salt and pepper.

3 Split and toast the muffins, and butter them just before serving.

4 Poach the eggs by bringing a saucepan of lightly salted water to the boil. Add the vinegar and reduce to a gentle simmer. Swirl the water with a fork and crack 2 of the eggs into the water. Cook for 3–4 minutes, remove carefully with a slotted spoon and repeat with the remaining 2 eggs.

5 Meanwhile, heat the hollandaise sauce according to the packet instructions.

6 Top the toasted muffins with some spinach and a poached egg and spoon over the hollandaise. Sprinkle with pepper and serve each egg with 3 asparagus spears on the side.

For eggs Benedict, an American brunch classic, replace the spinach with 8 rashers of grilled bacon or 4 slices of Parma ham.

family
favourites

spicy prawn & pea pilau

serves 4
prep + cook time 30 minutes

1 tablespoon sunflower oil
1 tablespoon butter
1 large onion, finely chopped
2 garlic cloves, finely chopped
1 tablespoon medium or hot curry
   paste
250 g (8 oz) basmati rice
600 ml (1 pint) hot fish or vegetable
   stock
300 g (10 oz) frozen peas
finely grated rind and juice of
   1 large lime
20 g (¾ oz) coriander, finely
   chopped
400 g (13 oz) cooked peeled
   prawns
salt and pepper

1 Heat the oil and butter in a heavy-based saucepan, add the onion and cook over a medium heat for 2–3 minutes until softened. Stir in the garlic and curry paste and cook for a further 1–2 minutes until fragrant, then add the rice and stir to coat well.
2 Stir in the stock, peas and lime rind, then season well and bring to the boil. Cover tightly, then reduce the heat to low and cook for 12–15 minutes or until the liquid is absorbed and the rice is tender.
3 Remove the pan from the heat, then stir in the lime juice, coriander and prawns. Cover and leave the prawns to heat through for a few minutes before serving.

Tip
You can use white or wholegrain basmati rice in this recipe. Wholegrain has the lowest GI (glycaemic index) of all types of rice.

sweet chilli salmon fishcakes

serves 2
prep + cook time 30 minutes + chilling time

250 g (8 oz) chunky boneless and skinless salmon fillet, roughly diced
1 tablespoon sweet chilli sauce
1 small garlic clove, crushed (optional)
2 spring onions, finely chopped
2 tablespoons finely chopped coriander
1 teaspoon finely grated lime rind (optional)
2 tablespoons vegetable oil

1 Place the diced salmon in a food processor with the chilli sauce, garlic, spring onions, coriander and lime rind and pulse quickly until chopped together, but not smooth. Scrape into a bowl, then use damp hands to shape into 2 patties. Arrange on a plate, cover with clingfilm and chill in the refrigerator for 10–12 minutes to firm up slightly.
2 Heat the oil in a large non-stick frying pan and cook the fishcakes over a medium heat for 5–6 minutes each side until golden and cooked through. Serve immediately with steamed or egg fried rice.

baked cod with tomatoes & olives

serves 4
prep + cook time 20 minutes

250 g (8 oz) cherry tomatoes,
    halved
100 g (3½ oz) pitted black olives
2 tablespoons capers in brine,
    drained
4 thyme sprigs, plus extra to
    garnish
4 cod fillets, about 175 g (6 oz)
    each
2 tablespoons extra virgin olive oil
2 tablespoons balsamic vinegar
salt and pepper

1 Combine the tomatoes, olives, capers and thyme sprigs in a roasting tin. Nestle the cod fillets in the pan, drizzle over the oil and balsamic vinegar and season to taste with salt and pepper.
2 Bake in a preheated oven, 200°C (400°F), Gas Mark 6, for 15 minutes.
3 Transfer the fish, tomatoes and olives to plates. Spoon the pan juices over the fish. Serve immediately with a mixed green leaf salad.

Tip
Try to buy sustainable cod which tastes better and helps to ensure that fish supplies don't run out.

tex-mex pork ribs with sweetcorn & red pepper salsa

serves 2
prep + cook time 30 minutes

3 tablespoons tomato ketchup
2 tablespoons soft brown sugar
2 tablespoons clear honey
1 tablespoon Worcestershire
   sauce
450 g (14½ oz) rack of mini pork
   ribs

sweetcorn & red pepper salsa
300 g (10 oz) canned sweetcorn,
   drained
1 red pepper, cored, deseeded
   and thinly sliced
1 bunch of spring onions, finely
   chopped
4 tablespoons chopped parsley
2 tablespoons olive oil
pepper

1 Mix together the ketchup, sugar, honey and Worcestershire sauce in a small bowl, then brush all over the ribs. Place the ribs in a large baking dish and bake in a preheated oven, 220°C (425°F), Gas Mark 7, for 25 minutes until golden and cooked through.
2 Meanwhile, make the salsa. Mix together all the ingredients in a bowl and season well with pepper.
3 Cut the pork into separate ribs and serve with the sweetcorn salsa.

garlicky pork with warm butter bean salad

serves 4
prep + cook time 20 minutes

4 tablespoons olive oil
2 garlic cloves, crushed
4 lean pork chops or steaks, about
    150 g (5 oz) each
salt and pepper

butter bean salad
2 tablespoons olive oil
2 x 400 g (13 oz) cans butter
    beans, rinsed and drained
12 cherry tomatoes, halved
150 ml (¼ pint) chicken stock
juice of 2 lemons
2 handfuls of parsley, chopped

1 For the pork, mix together the oil and garlic in a bowl, then season. Place the pork on a foil-lined grill rack and spoon over the garlicky oil. Cook under a preheated medium grill for about 10 minutes, turning occasionally, until golden and cooked through.

2 Meanwhile, make the salad. Heat the oil in a large frying pan, add the butter beans and tomatoes and heat through for a few minutes. Add the chicken stock, lemon juice and parsley and season. Serve with the grilled chops.

lamb hotpot

serves 4
prep + cook time 2 hours
30 minutes

8 lamb chops, about 1 kg (2 lb)
    total weight
50 g (2 oz) butter
1 tablespoon oil
2 teaspoons chopped rosemary
4 garlic cloves, sliced
2 onions, sliced
200 g (7 oz) chestnut mushrooms,
    halved
1 kg (2 lb) large potatoes, thinly
    sliced
450 ml (¾ pint) lamb stock
salt and pepper

1 Trim any excess fat from the lamb and season lightly on both sides with salt and pepper.

2 Melt half the butter with the oil in a shallow, flameproof casserole and fry the lamb in batches until browned. Drain to a plate.

3 Return the lamb chops to the casserole, arranging them side by side, and sprinkle with the rosemary and garlic. Tuck the onions and mushrooms around them, then place the potatoes on top. Pour the stock over.

4 Cover with a lid or foil and bake in a preheated oven, 160°C (325°F), Gas Mark 3, for 1½ hours. Dot with the remaining butter, return to the oven and cook, uncovered, for a further 45 minutes or until the potato topping is crisped and browned.

meatballs with tomato sauce

serves 4
prep + cook time 55 minutes

500 g (1 lb) lean minced beef
3 garlic cloves, crushed
2 small onions, finely chopped
25 g (1 oz) gluten-free
    breadcrumbs
40 g (1½ oz) freshly grated
    Parmesan cheese
6 tablespoons olive oil
100 ml (3½ fl oz) red wine
2 x 400 g (13 oz) cans chopped
    tomatoes
1 teaspoon caster sugar
3 tablespoons sun-dried tomato
    paste
75 g (3 oz) pitted Italian black
    olives, roughly chopped
4 tablespoons roughly chopped
    oregano
125 g (4 oz) mozzarella cheese,
    thinly sliced
salt and pepper

1 Put the beef in a bowl with half the crushed garlic and half the onion, the breadcrumbs and 25 g (1 oz) of the Parmesan. Season and use your hands to thoroughly blend the ingredients together. Shape into small balls, about 2.5 cm (1 inch) in diameter.

2 Heat half the oil in a large frying pan and fry the meatballs, shaking the pan frequently, for about 10 minutes until browned. Drain.

3 Add the remaining oil and onion to the pan and fry until softened. Add the wine and let the mixture bubble until the wine has almost evaporated. Stir in the remaining garlic, the tomatoes, sugar, tomato paste and a little seasoning. Bring to the boil and let the mixture bubble until slightly thickened.

4 Stir in the olives, all but 1 tablespoon of the oregano and the meatballs. Cook gently for a further 5 minutes.

5 Arrange the mozzarella slices over the top and scatter with the remaining oregano and Parmesan. Season with pepper and cook under a hot grill until the cheese starts to melt.

french-style chicken stew with tarragon

serves 4
prep + cook time 20 minutes

1 leek, trimmed and sliced
4 boneless, skinless chicken
    thighs, cut into chunks
400 g (13 oz) small new potatoes,
    halved
1 carrot, peeled and sliced
400 ml (14 fl oz) hot chicken stock
50 ml (2 fl oz) dry white wine
100 g (3½ oz) frozen peas, thawed
2 tablespoons crème fraîche
salt and pepper
handful of chopped tarragon,
    to serve

1 Place the leek, chicken, potatoes and carrot in a large saucepan. Pour in the stock and wine and season to taste.
2 Bring to the boil, then reduce the heat and simmer for 15 minutes until just cooked through.
3 Stir in the peas and crème fraîche and heat through. Scatter over the tarragon and serve immediately.

·

Tip
Tarragon has a distinctive liquorice-like flavour which goes well with chicken, fish, tomato and egg dishes.

chicken thighs with fresh pesto

serves 4
prep + cook time 30 minutes

1 tablespoon olive oil
8 boneless, skinless chicken
   thighs

pesto
90 ml (3 fl oz) olive oil
50 g (2 oz) pine nuts, toasted
50 g (2 oz) Parmesan cheese,
   freshly grated
50 g (2 oz) basil leaves, plus extra
   to garnish
15 g (½ oz) flat leaf parsley,
   roughly chopped
2 garlic cloves, chopped
salt and pepper

1 Heat the oil in a nonstick frying pan over a medium heat, add the chicken thighs and pan-fry gently, turning frequently, for 20 minutes or until cooked through.
2 To make the pesto, put all the ingredients in a blender or food processor and blend until smooth.
3 Remove the chicken from the pan and set aside to keep warm. Reduce the heat to as low as possible, add the pesto and heat through very gently for 2–3 minutes.
4 Pour the warmed pesto over the chicken thighs, garnish with extra basil and serve with roasted Mediterranean vegetables.

spanish turkey stew with lemon & chilli

serves 6
prep + cook time 30 minutes

800 g (1¾ lb) turkey breast steaks,
    cut into bite-sized pieces
2 tablespoons sunflower oil
4 garlic cloves, crushed
1 onion, finely chopped
2 teaspoons dried red chilli flakes
10–12 baby onions, peeled
2 carrots, peeled and cut into
    bite-sized pieces
2 potatoes, peeled and cut into
    bite-sized pieces
1 tablespoon sweet smoked
    paprika
3 tablespoons lemon juice
6 tablespoons finely chopped flat
    leaf parsley
500 ml (17 fl oz) hot chicken stock
salt and pepper

1 Season the turkey well. Heat the oil in a large frying pan, add the turkey and cook over a high heat, stirring occasionally, for 2–3 minutes or until browned all over.
2 Transfer to a heavy-based saucepan, stir in the remaining ingredients and bring to the boil. Reduce the heat to medium and cook, uncovered, for 20 minutes or until the turkey is cooked through and the vegetables are tender.
3 Ladle into bowls and serve.

potato pizza margherita

serves 3–4
prep + cook time 1 hour + cooling time

1 kg (2 lb) baking potatoes, peeled and cut into small chunks
3 tablespoons olive oil, plus extra for oiling
1 egg, beaten
50 g (2 oz) Parmesan or Cheddar cheese, grated
4 tablespoons sun-dried tomato paste or tomato ketchup
500 g (1 lb) small tomatoes, thinly sliced
125 g (4 oz) mozzarella cheese, thinly sliced
1 tablespoon chopped thyme, plus extra sprigs to garnish (optional)
salt

1 Cook the potatoes in a saucepan of salted boiling water for 15 minutes or until tender. Drain well, return to the pan and leave to cool for 10 minutes.

2 Add 2 tablespoons of the oil, the egg and half the grated Parmesan to the potato and mix well. Turn out on to an oiled baking sheet and spread out to form a 25 cm (10 inch) round. Place in a preheated oven, 200°C (400°F), Gas Mark 6, for 15 minutes.

3 Remove from the oven and spread with the tomato paste or ketchup. Arrange the tomato and mozzarella slices on top. Scatter with the remaining grated Parmesan, thyme, if using, and a little salt. Drizzle with the remaining oil.

4 Return to the oven for a further 15 minutes until the potato is crisp around the edges and the cheese is melting. Cut into generous wedges, garnish with thyme sprigs, if liked, and serve.

For corn & salami pizza, make as above, adding a 200 g (7 oz) can drained sweetcorn and 6 slices of chopped salami with the tomato and mozzarella to the top of the pizza. Continue as above.

tagliatelle with pumpkin & sage

serves 6
prep + cook time 30 minutes

875 g (1¾ lb) pumpkin, butternut
  or winter squash, peeled,
  deseeded and cut into 1.5 cm
  (¾ in) cubes
4 tablespoons olive oil
500 g (1 lb) fresh gluten-free
  tagliatelle
50 g (2 oz) rocket leaves
8 sage leaves, chopped
grated Parmesan cheese, to serve
  (optional)
salt and pepper

1 Place the pumpkin into a small roasting tin, add 2 tablespoons of the olive oil, season and toss to mix well. Roast in a preheated oven, 220°C (425°F), Gas Mark 7, for 15–20 minutes or until just tender.

2 Meanwhile, bring a large pan of salted water to the boil. Cook the pasta according to the packet instructions. Drain, return to the pan, then add the rocket, sage and pumpkin. Mix together over a gentle heat with the remaining olive oil until the rocket has wilted, then serve with a good grating of fresh Parmesan cheese, if desired.

chickpea & spinach curry

serves 4
prep + cook time 1 hour 20 minutes
+ soaking time

200 g (7 oz) dried chickpeas
2 tablespoons sunflower oil
2 onions, thinly sliced
2 teaspoons ground coriander
2 teaspoons ground cumin
1 teaspoon hot chilli powder
½ teaspoon ground turmeric
1 tablespoon medium curry powder
400 g (13 oz) canned chopped
   tomatoes
1 teaspoon soft brown sugar
100 ml (3½ fl oz) water
2 tablespoons chopped mint leaves
100 g (3½ oz) baby leaf spinach
salt
natural yogurt, to garnish (optional)

1 Soak the chickpeas in cold water overnight. Drain, rinse and place in a wok. Cover with water and bring to the boil. Reduce the heat and simmer for 45 minutes or until just tender. Drain and set aside.

2 Meanwhile, heat the oil in the wok, add the onions and cook over a low heat for 15 minutes until lightly golden. Add the coriander, cumin, chilli powder, turmeric and curry powder and stir-fry for 1–2 minutes.

3 Add the tomatoes, sugar and the measured water and bring to the boil. Cover, reduce the heat and simmer gently for 15 minutes.

4 Add the chickpeas, season well and cook gently for 8–10 minutes. Stir in the chopped mint. To serve, divide the spinach leaves among 4 shallow bowls and top with the chickpea mixture. Drizzle over some yogurt, if desired, and serve immediately with steamed rice.

roasted vegetable & potato bake

serves 4
prep + cook time 1 hour

1 tablespoon olive oil
200 g (7 oz) waxy potatoes, cut
   into chunks
1 yellow pepper, cored, deseeded
   and roughly diced
2 red peppers, cored, deseeded
   and roughly diced
4 garlic cloves, halved
2 tablespoons chopped thyme,
   plus extra sprigs to garnish
2 bay leaves
125 g (4 oz) feta cheese
2 tablespoons chopped mint
2 tablespoons chopped dill
50 g (2 oz) cream cheese
1 beefsteak tomato, roughly diced
200 g (7 oz) small courgettes,
   halved lengthways
salt and pepper

1 Toss the oil with the potatoes, peppers, garlic, thyme and bay leaves in an ovenproof serving dish and cook in a preheated oven, 200°C (400°F), Gas Mark 6, for 30 minutes.

2 Mash together the feta, mint, dill and cream cheese and season to taste.

3 Add the tomato and courgettes to the vegetables. Spoon the feta and cream cheese mixture over the vegetables and bake for a further 15 minutes until golden. Garnish with thyme sprigs and serve immediately, with a green salad.

food for
friends

rolled stuffed chicken breasts

serves 4

prep + cook time 30 minutes

4 boneless, skinless chicken
    breasts, about 150 g (5 oz) each
4 slices of Parma ham
4 thin slices of buffalo mozzarella
    cheese
4 asparagus tips, plus extra to
    serve
75 g (3 oz) gluten-free plain flour
1 tablespoon olive oil
50 g (2 oz) butter
50 ml (2 fl oz) dry white wine
75 ml (3 fl oz) chicken stock
200 g (7 oz) baby leaf spinach
200 g (7 oz) chilled pack sun-blush
    tomatoes in oil, drained
salt and pepper

1 Place each chicken breast between 2 sheets of greaseproof paper and flatten to about 2½ times its original size by pounding with a rolling pin.

2 Season the chicken with salt and pepper, place a slice of Parma ham, a slice of mozzarella and an asparagus tip on top and tightly roll up the chicken breasts. Tie with a piece of strong thread or spear with wooden cocktail sticks.

3 Season the flour with salt and pepper. Dip the prepared chicken rolls into the flour to coat evenly.

4 Heat the oil and half of the butter in a frying pan, add the chicken rolls and sauté over a low heat for 15 minutes or until golden all over and cooked through, turning frequently to brown the chicken evenly.

5 Remove the chicken, place in a serving dish and keep warm. Pour the wine and stock into the pan, bring to the boil and simmer for 3 minutes.

6 Remove the thread or cocktail sticks just before serving the chicken. Add the remaining butter to the pan, mix quickly with a small whisk to emulsify the sauce, add the spinach and tomatoes and cook for 2 minutes until the spinach has just wilted. Spoon on to plates, slice the chicken and arrange in a line down the centre.

Tip
If you can't find sun-blush tomatoes, serve this with roasted cherry tomatoes instead. Simply drizzle with a little olive oil and roast in a preheated oven, 180°C (350°F), Gas Mark 4, for 10–15 minutes.

duck breasts with lentils

serves 4
prep + cook time 40 minutes

4 x Barbary duck breasts, about
   175 g (6 oz) each
175 g (6 oz) puy lentils
150 ml (¼ pint) chicken stock
salt and pepper
chervil sprigs, to garnish

marmalade
300 ml (½ pint) orange juice
250 g (8 oz) mandarins, pips
   removed but with peel left on,
   finely chopped

sauce
3 shallots, finely chopped
50 ml (2 fl oz) port
150 ml (¼ pint) red grape juice

1 Put the duck breasts in a shallow roasting tray, skin side up, and roast in a preheated oven, 200°C (400°F), Gas Mark 6, for 10–15 minutes – they should still be pink in the centre. Leave to rest for 5 minutes.

2 Meanwhile, put the lentils in a saucepan of salted water, bring to the boil and boil for 15 minutes, then drain.

3 While the duck and lentils are cooking, make the marmalade. Put the orange juice and mandarins in a stainless-steel saucepan. Bring to the boil, then reduce the heat and cook for 10 minutes, or until reduced by two-thirds. At the same time, for the sauce, heat a dry nonstick frying pan, add the shallots and cook gently for 2–3 minutes. Add the port and grape juice. Bring to the boil and boil for 10 minutes, or until reduced by half.

4 Remove the duck from the pan and set aside. Skim off the excess fat from the pan. Add the cooked lentils and stock and cook over a medium heat, scraping any residue from the pan, for 2–3 minutes until the stock has nearly all evaporated.

5 Slice the duck. Divide the lentils among serving plates and top with the duck slices. Spoon a little marmalade over the meat, pour the sauce around the lentils and serve garnished with chervil sprigs.

balsamic chicken with root veg

serves 4
prep + cook time 1 hour 10 minutes
+ marinating time

4 chicken thighs, skinned
4 chicken drumsticks, skinned
3 tablespoons balsamic vinegar
3 tablespoons white wine
small bunch fresh sage
550 g (1 lb 2 oz) potatoes,
    scrubbed and cut into wedges
275 g (9 oz) parsnips, peeled and
    cut into wedges
275 g (9 oz) baby carrots,
    scrubbed and halved
    lengthways
2 small red onions, cut into
    wedges
4 tablespoons olive oil
salt and pepper

1 Slash each chicken piece 2 or 3 times with a small knife then put into a large plastic bag with the balsamic vinegar, wine, sage and some seasoning. Seal the bag well and chill for 3–4 hours or until required.

2 Cook the potatoes in a saucepan of boiling water for 4–5 minutes until almost tender, then drain well and tip into a large roasting tin. Add the parsnips, carrots and onion wedges. Tip in the chicken and the marinade, drizzle the oil over the vegetables and sprinkle with a little seasoning.

3 Roast in a preheated oven, 200°C (400°F), Gas Mark 6, for 40–45 minutes, turning the vegetables once or twice until golden and the juices run clear when the chicken is pierced with a small knife. Serve with a mixed leaf salad.

Tip
This makes a relaxed Sunday lunch. You can vary the vegetables, depending on what you have. Try sweet potato instead of the potato and butternut squash instead of the parsnips.

spiced chicken stew with preserved lemon

serves 4
prep + cook time 30 minutes

2 tablespoons olive oil
800 g (1¾ lb) boneless, skinless
    chicken breasts, cut into
    bite-sized pieces
1 large onion, thinly sliced
4 garlic cloves, finely chopped
1 teaspoon peeled and finely
    grated fresh root ginger
1 red chilli, deseeded and finely
    chopped
2 teaspoons ground cumin
3 cinnamon sticks
¼ teaspoon ground turmeric
2 large carrots, peeled and cut into
    bite-sized pieces
large pinch of saffron threads
750 ml (1¼ pints) hot chicken
    stock
1 tablespoon rose harissa paste
8 green olives, pitted
8 black olives, pitted
6 small preserved lemons, halved
salt and pepper

1 Heat the oil in a large heavy-based saucepan, add the chicken and onion and cook over a high heat, stirring occasionally, for 2–3 minutes until browned. Add the garlic, ginger, red chilli, cumin, cinnamon sticks and turmeric and fry, stirring, for 30 seconds.

2 Add the carrots, saffron and stock and bring to the boil. Reduce the heat to medium and cook, uncovered, for 15–20 minutes or until the chicken is cooked through and the carrots are tender.

3 Add the harissa, olives and preserved lemons, season to taste and stir to mix well. Ladle into bowls and serve immediately.

Tip
Preserved lemons
are a speciality of
North African and
Middle Eastern cuisine
and are especially good
with lamb or fish
dishes.

seafood stew with gremolata

serves 4
prep + cook time 1 hour 10 minutes

½ teaspoon saffron threads
2 tablespoons boiling water
3 tablespoons olive oil
1 onion, roughly chopped
2 yellow peppers, quartered,
    deseeded and thickly sliced
400 g (13 oz) can chopped
    tomatoes
150 ml (¼ pint) fish stock
200 ml (7 fl oz) dry white wine
2 tablespoons sun-dried tomato
    paste
400 g (13 oz) baby new potatoes,
    scrubbed
4 tablespoons roughly chopped
    flat-leaf parsley
finely grated rind of 1 lemon
1–2 garlic cloves, finely chopped
625 g (1¼ lb) cod loin, cut into
    large cubes
250 g (8 oz) mixed shellfish
    and squid
salt and pepper

1 Put the saffron into a small cup, cover with the boiling water and leave to soak.

2 Heat the oil in a flameproof casserole, add the onion and peppers and fry gently for 5 minutes until just beginning to brown. Stir in the tomatoes, fish stock and wine. Mix in the tomato paste and some seasoning, then add the potatoes and saffron with its soaking water. Bring to the boil then cover and simmer for 20 minutes until the potatoes are just tender. Meanwhile make the gremolata.

3 To make the gremolata, mix together the parsley, lemon rind and garlic, cover and chill until required.

4 Add the cod and seafood to the casserole dish. Cover and simmer gently for 15 minutes until the cod is just tender. Be careful not to overcook or the cod will fall apart. Sprinkle with a little of the gremolata, then ladle into shallow bowls. Serve immediately with warm gluten-free bread, salad and the remaining gremolata for sprinkling.

asparagus, lemon & herb-stuffed salmon

serves 4
prep + cook time 30 minutes

20 fine asparagus spears, trimmed
butter, for greasing
8 pieces of salmon fillet, about
   125 g (4 oz) each, skinned
finely grated rind and juice of
   1 lemon
4 tablespoons chopped parsley
2 tablespoons chopped dill
salt and pepper

1 Cook the asparagus in a large saucepan of lightly salted boiling water for 3–4 minutes until just tender. Drain well.

2 Lightly grease a baking sheet, then place 4 salmon fillets on the sheet, skinned side up. Toss the asparagus with the lemon rind, parsley and dill and season well. Arrange on top of the salmon fillets, then top with the remaining salmon fillets, skinned side down. Using 3 pieces of kitchen string on each, roughly tie the salmon pieces together to enclose the filling. Season and pour over the lemon juice.

3 Place in a preheated oven, 220°C (425°F), Gas Mark 7, for 10 minutes, or until the fish is opaque and cooked through. Serve with new potatoes and salad, if liked.

Tip
Heart-healthy salmon is rich in omega-3 fats. For maximum health benefits, aim to eat 2–3 portions of oily fish each week.

oysters rockefeller

serves 4
prep + cook time 30 minutes

3 tablespoons olive oil
1 shallot, diced
1 garlic clove, crushed
175 g (6 oz) baby spinach leaves
dash of Pernod (optional)
rock salt
24 oysters, opened and in the
    half-shells
100 g (3½ oz) fresh gluten-free
    wholemeal breadcrumbs
100 g (3½ oz) Parmesan cheese,
    grated

1 Heat 2 tablespoons of the oil in a frying pan, add the shallot and garlic and cook for 2–3 minutes. Add the spinach and stir until wilted. Add the Pernod, if using, and cook until the liquid has been absorbed.
2 Cover the base of a roasting tin with rock salt, then arrange the oysters on top. Spoon the spinach mixture on to the oysters. Mix together the breadcrumbs and cheese, then sprinkle over the spinach.
3 Drizzle with the remaining oil and bake in a preheated oven, 200°C (400°F), Gas Mark 6, for 10–15 minutes until lightly golden.

Tip
Named after John D Rockefeller, one of the wealthiest men in the world and a noted philanthropist, this dish originated in New Orleans.

lamb stuffed with rice & peppers

serves 4
prep + cook time 2 hours

2 red peppers, cored, deseeded
 and halved
50 g (2 oz) wild rice, cooked
5 garlic cloves, chopped
5 semi-dried tomatoes, chopped
2 tablespoons chopped flat leaf
 parsley
625 g (1¼ lb) boneless leg of
 lamb, butterflied
salt and pepper
4 artichoke halves

1 Put the pepper halves in a roasting tin and cook in a preheated oven, 180°C (350°F), Gas Mark 4, for 20 minutes, until the skin has blackened and blistered. Cover with damp kitchen paper and set aside. When the peppers are cool enough to handle, peel off the skin and chop the flesh. Do not turn off the oven.

2 Mix together one of the chopped peppers, the rice, garlic, tomatoes and parsley. Season to taste.

3 Put the lamb on a board and make a horizontal incision, almost all the way along, to make a cavity for stuffing. Fold back the top half, spoon in the stuffing and fold back the top. Secure with skewers.

4 Cook the lamb for 1 hour, basting frequently. Add the artichokes and other pepper for the last 15 minutes of cooking time. Slice the lamb and serve immediately with roasted new potatoes, if liked.

bangkok sour pork curry

serves 4
prep + cook time 2 hours
20 minutes

1 tablespoon sunflower oil
1 onion, finely chopped
1 teaspoon finely grated galangal
 or fresh root ginger
3 tablespoons Thai red curry paste
750 g (1½ lb) thick pork steaks, cut
 into bite-sized pieces
750 ml (1¼ pints) chicken stock
8 tablespoons finely chopped
 fresh coriander stems
2 lemon grass stalks, bruised
4 tablespoons tamarind paste
1 tablespoon grated palm sugar
6 lime leaves

to garnish
small handful Thai basil leaves
fresh lime leaves (optional)

1 Heat the oil in a large, heavy-based casserole dish and fry the onion over a medium heat for 3–4 minutes. Add the galangal or ginger, curry paste and pork and stir-fry for 4–5 minutes.
2 Pour in the stock and add the chopped coriander, lemon grass, tamarind, palm sugar and lime leaves. Bring to the boil, remove from the heat, cover and cook in a preheated oven at 150°C (300°F), Gas Mark 2 for 2 hours or until the pork is tender.
3 Scatter over the basil leaves just before serving and garnish with lime leaves, if liked. Serve with steamed jasmine rice.

spiced lamb with bean purée

serves 2–3
prep + cook time 1 hour 10 minutes
+ resting time

2 large baking potatoes, cut into
   1.5 cm (¾ inch) pieces
4 tablespoons olive oil
40 g (1½ oz) gluten-free
   breadcrumbs
1 garlic clove, crushed
2 tablespoons chopped fresh
   coriander
1 teaspoon ground coriander
1 teaspoon ground cumin
1 egg yolk
1 rack of lamb, chined and
   trimmed
4 large flat mushrooms
150 g (5 oz) frozen baby broad
   beans
1 tablespoon chopped mint
100 ml (3½ fl oz) white wine
salt and pepper

1 Toss the potatoes with 2 tablespoons of the oil and salt and pepper in a small, sturdy roasting pan. Roast in a preheated oven, 200°C (400°F), Gas Mark 6, for 15 minutes.

2 Mix together the breadcrumbs, garlic, fresh coriander, spices and seasoning. Cut away any thick areas of fat from the skinned side of the lamb. Brush the lamb with the egg yolk and spoon the breadcrumb mixture over, pressing down gently with the back of the spoon. Brush the mushrooms with the remaining oil and a little seasoning.

3 Turn the potatoes in the pan and add the lamb, crusted-side uppermost. Return to the oven for 30 minutes. (The cutlets will still be slightly pink in the middle after this time, so cook for a little longer if you prefer them well done.) After 15 minutes of the cooking time, turn the potatoes in the oil and add the mushrooms. Return to the oven for the remaining cooking time.

4 Drain the meat to a board. Cover with foil and leave to rest for 15 minutes. Transfer the potatoes and mushrooms to a serving dish.

5 Add the broad beans, mint and wine to the roasting pan and cook over a gentle heat for 5 minutes until the beans are tender. Tip into a blender or food processor and blend until smooth. Check the seasoning and spoon on to serving plates. Carve the lamb into cutlets and add to the plates with the mushrooms and potatoes.

Tip
To chine – or French trim – a rack of lamb, means removing the meat, fat and membranes that connect the rib bones, giving the rack a clean appearance.

creamy pea & mint risotto with brie

serves 4
prep + cook time 50 minutes

1.2 litres (2 pints) vegetable stock
50 g (2 oz) butter
1 large onion, finely chopped
2 garlic cloves, crushed
300 g (10 oz) arborio rice
150 ml (¼ pint) dry white wine
350 g (11½ oz) fresh or frozen
   shelled peas
½ bunch fresh mint leaves, torn
50 g (2 oz) Brie, diced
salt and pepper
freshly grated Parmesan cheese,
   to serve

1 Put the stock in a saucepan and bring to a very gentle simmer.
2 Meanwhile, melt the butter in a saucepan, add the onion, garlic and salt and pepper and cook over a low heat, stirring occasionally, for 10 minutes until the onion is softened but not browned. Add the rice and cook, stirring, for 1 minute until all the grains are glossy. Stir in the wine, bring to the boil and continue to boil for 1–2 minutes until absorbed. Stir in the peas.
3 Stir about 150 ml (¼ pint) of the stock into the rice. Cook over a medium heat, stirring constantly, until absorbed. Continue to add the stock, a little at a time, and cook, stirring constantly, for about 20 minutes until the rice is al dente and the stock has all been absorbed.
4 Remove the pan from the heat. Stir in the mint and Brie, cover and leave to stand for 5 minutes until the cheese has melted. Serve with grated Parmesan.

melanzane parmigiana

serves 4
prep + cook time 1 hour 30 minutes
+ standing time

6 aubergines
2 tablespoons olive oil
250 g (8 oz) grated Cheddar
   cheese
50 g (2 oz) grated Parmesan
   cheese

tomato sauce
2 tablespoons olive oil
1 large onion, chopped
2 garlic cloves, finely chopped
14 oz can chopped tomatoes
salt and pepper

1 Make the tomato sauce, by first heating the olive oil in a frying pan. Fry the onion for 5 minutes, then add the garlic and the tomatoes and cook, gently, for 10 minutes. Season well and keep warm.

2 Trim the ends off the aubergines and cut them lengthways into thick slices. Sprinkle generously with salt and set side for about 10 minutes. Wash well, drain and pat dry on kitchen paper.

3 Brush the aubergine slices with oil, and place them on 2 large baking sheets. Roast the aubergines in a preheated oven, 200°C (400°F), Gas Mark 6, for 10 minutes on each side until golden and tender. Do not turn off the oven.

4 Spoon a little of the tomato sauce into an ovenproof dish, and top with a layer of roasted aubergine and some of the Cheddar. Continue with the layers, finishing with the Cheddar. Sprinkle over the Parmesan, and bake for 30 minutes until bubbling and golden. Remove from the oven, and leave to stand for 5–10 minutes. Serve with a crisp green salad.

cakes & bakes

nutty seed loaf

serves 8
prep + cook time 35 minutes + cooling time

400 g (13 oz) brown rice flour, plus extra for dusting
25 g (1 oz) rice bran
2 tablespoons dried milk powder
½ teaspoon bicarbonate of soda
1 teaspoon gluten-free baking powder
½–1 teaspoon salt
1 teaspoon xanthan gum
pinch of caster sugar
50 g (2 oz) mixed seeds, such as sunflower and pumpkin
50 g (2 oz) hazelnuts, toasted and roughly chopped
1 egg, lightly beaten
300 ml (½ pint) buttermilk

1 Place all the dry ingredients, including the nuts, in a large bowl and mix together. In a separate bowl, mix together the egg and buttermilk, then stir into the dry ingredients.
2 Tip the dough out on to a surface dusted lightly with rice flour and form into a round about 20 cm (8 inches) in diameter. Mark into eight segments, then place on a baking sheet and dust with a little extra flour.
3 Place in an oven preheated to its highest setting and cook for 10 minutes, then reduce the heat to 200°C (400°F), Gas Mark 6, and continue to cook for about 15 minutes until the loaf is golden and sounds hollow when tapped.
4 Remove the loaf from the oven and transfer to a wire rack to cool.

Tip
Pronounced 'zan-than', xanthan gum has a neutral flavour and is indispensable for the gluten-free baker.

feta & herb loaf

serves 14
prep + cook time 55 minutes + proving and cooling time

200 g (7 oz) polenta
100 g (3½ oz) rice flour
50 g (2 oz) dried milk powder
pinch of salt
7 g (¼ oz) sachet fast-action dried yeast
2 teaspoons caster sugar
2 teaspoons xanthan gum
3 eggs, beaten
2 tablespoons chopped mixed herbs
450 ml (¾ pint) tepid water
100 g (3½ oz) feta cheese, crumbled

1 Grease and line a 1 kg (2 lb) loaf tin. Sift the polenta, flour, milk powder and salt into a large bowl and stir well to combine. Stir in the yeast, sugar and xanthan gum.
2 Place the eggs, herbs and measured water in a bowl and mix together. Stir this mixture into the dry ingredients and combine to form a soft dough. Beat for 5 minutes, then stir in the feta cheese.
3 Spoon the mixture into the prepared tin, cover with a clean damp tea towel and leave in a warm place to rise for about 30 minutes, until the mixture is near the top of the tin. Place in a preheated oven, 180°C (350°F), Gas Mark 4, for about 45 minutes until brown and hollow-sounding when tapped.
4 Remove the loaf from the oven and transfer to a wire rack to cool.

perfect pecan pies

makes 8
prep + cook time 35 minutes + chilling and cooling time

75 g (3 oz) brown rice flour, plus extra for dusting
50 g (2 oz) gram flour
75 g (3 oz) polenta
1 teaspoon xanthan gum
125 g (4 oz) butter, cubed
2 tablespoons caster sugar
1 egg, beaten

filling
100 g (3½ oz) light muscovado sugar
150 g (5 oz) butter
125 g (4 oz) honey
175 g (6 oz) pecan halves, half of them roughly chopped
2 eggs, beaten

1 Place the flours, polenta, xanthan gum and butter in a food processor and whiz until the mixture resembles fine breadcrumbs, or rub in by hand in a large bowl. Stir in the sugar.

2 Add the egg and very gently mix in using a knife, adding enough cold water (probably a couple of teaspoons) to make a dough. Try not to let it become too wet. Knead for a couple of minutes, then wrap closely in clingfilm and chill for about an hour.

3 Meanwhile, place the sugar, butter and honey for the filling in a medium saucepan and heat until the sugar has dissolved. Leave to cool for 10 minutes.

4 Remove the dough from the refrigerator while the filling is cooking. Knead it on a surface dusted lightly with rice flour to soften it a little. Divide the dough into eight, then roll each piece out to a thickness of 2.5 mm (⅛ inch). Use to line eight individual 11.5 cm (4½ inch) pie tins, rolling the rolling pin over the top to cut off the excess dough.

5 Stir the chopped pecans and eggs into the filling mixture and pour into the pastry-lined tins. Arrange the pecan halves over the top, then place in a preheated oven, 200°C (400°F), Gas Mark 6, for 15–20 minutes until the filling is firm. Remove the pies and leave to cool.

crispy cornbread

serves 4
prep + cook time 30 minutes + cooling time

15 g (½ oz) lard
15 g (½ oz) butter, melted
1 tablespoon vegetable oil
2 spring onions, diced
1 red chilli, deseeded and diced
125 g (4 oz) sweetcorn
150 g (5 oz) polenta
15 g (½ oz) plain gluten-free flour
2 teaspoons gluten-free baking powder
1 teaspoon bicarbonate of soda
pinch of salt
2 teaspoons caster sugar
1 egg, beaten
175 ml (6 fl oz) buttermilk

1 Grease a 20 cm (8 inch) round cake tin with the lard and place in a preheated oven, 200°C (400°F), Gas Mark 6, to heat.
2 Place the butter and oil in a frying pan over a medium heat, add the spring onions, chilli and sweetcorn and cook for 1 minute, then remove from the heat.
3 In a large bowl, sift together the polenta, flour, baking powder, bicarbonate of soda, salt and sugar. Make a well in the centre.
4 Beat together the egg and buttermilk, then pour into the well and gradually bring the mixture together with a fork. Stir in the spring onion mixture.
5 Remove the cake tin from the oven and pour in the corn mixture. Return to the oven and bake for 20–23 minutes, until golden.
6 Cool on a wire rack and cut into wedges to serve.

Tip
Despite its name, buttermilk contains no butter. It has a slightly tart taste and is excellent for making scones and breads such as soda bread and this cornbread.

chocolate biscuit cake

makes 8 slices

prep time 15 minutes + cooling and
chilling time

300 g (10 oz) plain chocolate,
   broken into pieces

2 tablespoons milk

125 g (4 oz) butter, melted, plus
   extra for greasing

125 g (4 oz) gluten-free digestive
   biscuits, lightly crushed

2 packets white chocolate buttons

2 packets milk chocolate buttons

1 Grease an 18 cm (7 inch) round cake tin or similar. Put the plain chocolate and milk in a bowl set over a pan of simmering water, making sure the bowl does not touch the water, and leave until the chocolate has melted, stirring occasionally. Stir in the butter. Remove the bowl from the heat and leave until cool, but not solid.

2 Mix the biscuit pieces with the white and milk chocolate buttons, then stir the mixture into the melted chocolate, pour it into the tin and squash it down gently. Put in the refrigerator for at least 3 hours until firm, then cut into wedges.

choc chip cookies

makes 30
prep + cook time 20 minutes + cooling time

75 g (3 oz) butter
100 g (3½ oz) golden caster sugar
75 g (3 oz) soft light brown sugar
1 egg, beaten
150 g (5 oz) brown rice flour, plus extra for dusting
½ teaspoon bicarbonate of soda
1 tablespoon cocoa powder
75 g (3 oz) plain dark chocolate chips

1 Whizz all the ingredients except the chocolate chips in a food processor until smooth, or beat in a large bowl. Stir in the chocolate chips, and bring the mixture together with your hands to form a ball.
2 Dust a surface lightly with rice flour. On this, divide the mixture into 30 balls, then place them, well spaced apart, on baking sheets lined with nonstick baking paper. Press them down gently with the back of a fork.
3 Bake in a preheated oven,180°C (350°F), Gas Mark 4, for 8–10 minutes. Remove the cookies from the oven, leave for a few minutes to harden, then transfer to a wire rack to cool.

For choc & cherry cookies replace the caster with light muscovado sugar and whizz in a processor with the other ingredients. Stir in 50 g (2 oz) plain dark chocolate chips and 50 g (2 oz) dried sour cherries, then proceed as above.

lemon & poppyseed muffins

makes 12
prep + cook time 30 minutes + cooling time

2 tablespoons clear honey
2 tablespoons poppy seeds
juice of 2 lemons, plus the grated rind of 1 lemon
110 g (3½ oz) unsalted butter, melted
110 g (3½ oz) caster sugar
2 eggs
175 g (6 oz) natural yogurt
350 g (11½ oz) self-raising gluten-free flour
1 teaspoon gluten-free baking powder
½ teaspoon bicarbonate of soda

1 Line a 12-hole muffin tin with paper cases.
2 Place the honey in a small saucepan over a medium heat and add the poppy seeds, the lemon rind and half the lemon juice. Heat until the honey is melted, then take off the heat and pour into a bowl. Stir in the remaining lemon juice and leave to cool for 1–2 minutes.
3 Whisk in the melted butter, sugar, eggs and yogurt.
4 Sift the flour, baking powder and bicarbonate of soda into a large bowl and pour in the yogurt mixture. Gently mix together until just combined – do not overmix.
5 Divide among the paper muffin cases and bake in a preheated oven, 190°C (375°F), Gas Mark 5, for 15–18 minutes, until golden. Cool on a wire rack.

Tip
Resist the temptation to overmix the muffins. Too much stirring will result in muffins with a dense texture that don't rise as much as they should.

lemon drizzle loaf

serves 12
prep + cook time 55 minutes +
cooling time

250 g (8 oz) butter, softened, plus
   extra for greasing
250 g (8 oz) caster sugar
250 g (8 oz) brown rice flour
2 teaspoons gluten-free baking
   powder
4 eggs, beaten
grated rind and juice of 1 lemon
lemon rind twist, to decorate
   (optional)

lemon drizzle
grated rind and juice of 2 lemons
100 g (3½ oz) granulated sugar

1 Grease and line a 900 g (2 lb) loaf tin.
2 Place all the cake ingredients in a food processor and whizz until
smooth or beat together in a large bowl until light and fluffy.
3 Spoon the mixture into the prepared tin and place in a preheated
oven, 180°C (350°F), Gas Mark 4, for 35–40 minutes until golden and
firm to the touch. Remove from the oven and transfer to a wire rack.
4 Prick holes all over the sponge with a cocktail stick. Mix together
the drizzle ingredients in a bowl, then drizzle the liquid over the warm
loaf. Leave until completely cold. Decorate with a twist of lemon rind,
if liked.

almond angel cakes with berries

makes 6
prep + cook time 30 minutes +
cooling time

4 egg whites
3 tablespoons granulated sugar
50 g (2 oz) ground almonds
generous pinch of cream of tartar
15 g (½ oz) flaked almonds
1 tablespoon sifted icing sugar, to
   dust (optional)

berries with fromage frais
200 g (7 oz) fromage frais
2 tablespoons clear honey or
   sifted icing sugar (optional)
400 g (13 oz) frozen mixed berry
   fruits, just thawed

1 Brush 6 holes of a deep muffin tin with a little sunflower oil and line the bases with rounds of greaseproof paper. Whisk the egg whites in a clean, dry bowl until stiff, moist peaks form. Whisk in the granulated sugar, a teaspoonful at a time, until it has all been added. Keep whisking for 1–2 minutes until thick and glossy.

2 Fold in the ground almonds and cream of tartar, then spoon the mixture into the prepared sections of the muffin tin. Sprinkle the flaked almonds over the top of each one. Bake in a preheated oven, 180°C (350°F), Gas Mark 4, for 10–12 minutes until golden brown and set. Carefully loosen the edges of the cakes with a knife, then lift on to a wire rack to cool.

3 Put the fromage frais in a bowl and stir through the honey or icing sugar to sweeten, if liked. Swirl the thawed berry fruits through the fromage frais. Arrange the angel cakes on a serving plate, dusted with the icing sugar, if liked. Serve with the swirled fruits and fromage frais for spooning over.

Tip
A by-product of winemaking – it is derived from the crystals that form inside wine barrels – cream of tartar is used in baking to add volume to beaten egg whites.

chocolate almond torte

serves 16
prep + cook time 1 hour 35 minutes
+ cooling time

200 g (7 oz) plain dark chocolate
5 large eggs
125 g (4 oz) golden caster sugar
100 g (3½ oz) ground almonds
1 tablespoon coffee liqueur
cocoa powder, for dusting
200 g (7 oz) fresh raspberries

1 Melt the chocolate in a bowl over a pan of simmering water.
2 Separate all but one of the eggs, reserving the whites. Whisk the remaining whole egg, egg yolks and sugar in a bowl until the mixture is thick and pale and leaves a trail when the beaters are lifted.
3 Whisk in the melted chocolate slowly and then add the almonds. Clean the beaters and whisk the egg whites to soft peaks. Whisk one-quarter of the egg whites into the mix to loosen, then fold in the rest.
4 Grease and line a round cake tin, 12 cm (5 inches) in diameter and 8 cm (3½ inches) deep, ensuring the nonstick baking paper comes about 7 cm (3 inches) above the tin. Pour the mixture into the tin and bake in a preheated oven, 160°C (325°F), Gas Mark 3, for 1–1¼ hours or until a skewer inserted into the centre of the cake comes out clean.
5 Make several holes in the cake while still hot and drizzle over the coffee liqueur. Cool in the tin for 30 minutes. To serve, place the cake on a stand, dust with cocoa powder, top with a pile of raspberries and wrap a wide ribbon around it, if liked.

mini chocolate meringues

makes 6
prep + cook time 1 hour 30 minutes
+ cooling time

3 egg whites
75 g (3 oz) golden caster sugar
75 g (3 oz) light muscovado sugar
75 g (3 oz) milk chocolate, grated

1 Whisk the egg whites in a clean bowl until stiffly peaking. Whisk in the golden caster sugar 1 tablespoon at a time, then whisk in the light muscovado sugar, also 1 tablespoon at a time. Fold in the chocolate.

2 Line 2 baking sheets with nonstick baking paper. Drop teaspoonfuls of the meringue mixture on to the baking sheets.

3 Bake in a preheated oven to 140°C (275°F), Gas Mark 1, for 1¼ hours, then turn off the heat and leave in the oven for another 30 minutes.

coconut & mango cake

serves 12
prep + cook time 1 hour + cooling time

100 g (3½ oz) butter, softened, plus extra for greasing
100 g (3½ oz) soft light brown sugar
4 eggs, separated
400 ml (14 fl oz) buttermilk
200 g (7 oz) polenta
200 g (7 oz) rice flour
2 teaspoons gluten-free baking powder
50 g (2 oz) coconut milk powder
50 g (2 oz) desiccated coconut
1 mango, peeled, stoned and puréed

filling
250 g (8 oz) mascarpone cheese
1 mango, peeled, stoned and finely chopped
2 tablespoons icing sugar

1 Grease and line a 23 cm (9 inch) round deep cake tin.
2 Beat together the butter and sugar in a large bowl until light and fluffy, then beat in the egg yolks, buttermilk, polenta, flour, baking powder, coconut milk powder and desiccated coconut.
3 Whisk the egg whites in a large clean bowl until they form soft peaks, then fold into the cake mixture with the puréed mango.
4 Spoon the mixture into the prepared tin and place in a preheated oven, 200°C (400°F), Gas Mark 6, for 45–50 minutes until golden and firm to the touch. Remove from the oven and transfer to a wire rack to cool.
5 Slice the cake in half horizontally, when cool. Beat together the filling ingredients in a bowl and use half to sandwich the cakes together. Smooth the remaining mixture over the top.

Tip
When choosing a mango, don't judge it by its colour – red does not necessarily indicate that it's ripe. Squeeze gently to judge for ripeness.

beetroot speckled cake

serves 10
prep + cook time 1 hour + cooling time

200 g (7 oz) butter, melted, plus extra for greasing
200 g (7 oz) soft light brown sugar
200 g (7 oz) raw beetroot, peeled and grated
150 g (5 oz) whole mixed nuts, toasted and chopped
3 eggs, separated
1 teaspoon gluten-free baking powder
½ teaspoon ground cinnamon
grated rind and juice of 1 orange
200 g (7 oz) rice flour
3 tablespoons ground almonds

to decorate
200 g (7 oz) cream cheese
1 tablespoon icing sugar
150 g (5 oz) whole mixed nuts

1 Grease a 20 cm (8 inch) round deep cake tin.
2 Whisk together the melted butter and sugar in a large bowl until pale. Stir in the beetroot, two-thirds of the nuts and the egg yolks.
3 Stir together the baking powder, cinnamon, orange rind and juice, flour and ground almonds in a separate bowl. Add to the beetroot mixture and beat until smooth.
4 Whisk the egg whites in a large clean bowl until they form soft peaks, then fold into the beetroot mixture.
5 Spoon the mixture into the prepared tin and place in a preheated oven, 200°C (400°F), Gas Mark 6, for 45–50 minutes until firm to the touch. Remove from the oven and transfer to a wire rack to cool.
6 Beat together the cream cheese and icing sugar in a bowl, then smooth the icing over the top of the cooled cake. Decorate with the whole nuts.

For chocolate beetroot cake, make the cake mixture as above and fold in 100 g (3½ oz) chopped plain dark chocolate. Bake as above and leave to cool. Top the cake with grated plain dark chocolate.

delicious
desserts

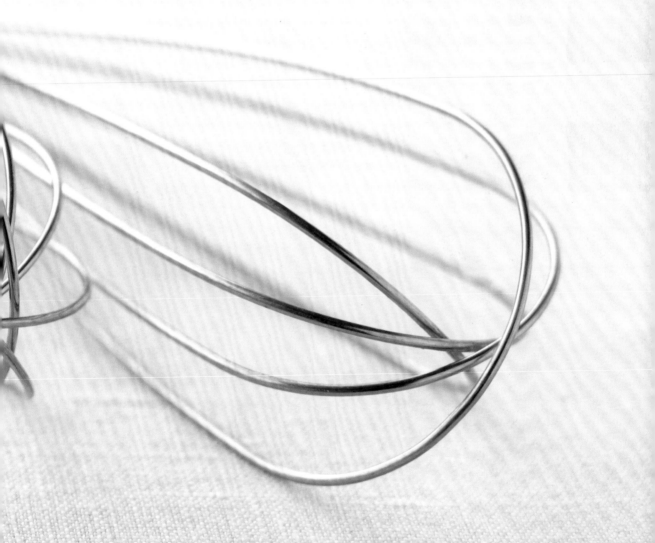

chocolate & chestnut roulade

serves 8
prep + cook time 45 minutes + cooling time

125 g (4 oz) plain dark chocolate, broken into pieces
5 eggs, separated
175 g (6 oz) caster sugar, plus extra to sprinkle
2 tablespoons cocoa powder, sifted
250 g (8 oz) canned unsweetened chestnut purée
4 tablespoons icing sugar
1 tablespoon brandy
250 ml (8 fl oz) double cream
icing sugar, for dusting

1 Melt the chocolate, then leave to cool for 5 minutes. Put the egg yolks in a bowl, add the sugar and whisk together for 5 minutes until pale and thickened. Stir in the melted chocolate and cocoa. Whisk the egg whites in a clean bowl until stiff and fold into the chocolate mixture until evenly combined.

2 Grease and line a 33 x 23 cm (13 x 9 inch) Swiss roll tin. Transfer the mixture to the tin, spreading it well into the corners, and smooth the surface with a palette knife. Bake in a preheated oven, 180°C (350°F), Gas Mark 4, for 20 minutes until risen and set.

3 Sprinkle a large sheet of baking paper with caster sugar. Remove the roulade from the oven and turn it out immediately on to the sugared paper. Carefully remove the lining paper and cover the roulade with a clean tea towel. Set aside to cool.

4 Put the chestnut purée and icing sugar in a food processor and purée until smooth (or combine well by hand). Transfer the mixture to a bowl and stir in the brandy. Gently whisk in the cream until light and fluffy. Spread the filling over the roulade, leaving a 1 cm (½ inch) border, and roll it up from one short end to form a log. Serve dusted with sifted icing sugar.

Tip
Using both hands, use the baking paper underneath to help you gently roll the roulade into shape. Don't worry if it cracks – it's supposed to!

chocolate ice cream

serves 4
prep + cook time 30 minutes +
cooling and freezing time

300 ml (½ pint) double cream
2 tablespoons milk
50 g (2 oz) icing sugar, sifted
½ teaspoon vanilla essence
125 g (4 oz) good-quality plain dark
   chocolate, broken into pieces
2 tablespoons single cream

chocolate sauce (optional)
150 ml (¼ pint) water
3 tablespoons caster sugar
150 g (5 oz) plain dark chocolate,
   broken into pieces

1 Put the double cream and milk in a bowl and whisk until just stiff. Stir in the icing sugar and vanilla essence. Pour the mixture into a shallow freezer container and freeze for 30 minutes or until the ice cream begins to set around the edges. (This ice cream cannot be made in an ice-cream machine.)
2 Melt the chocolate, together with the single cream, over a pan of gently simmering water. Stir until smooth, then set aside to cool.
3 Remove the ice cream from the freezer and spoon into a bowl. Add the melted chocolate and quickly stir it through the ice cream with a fork. Return the ice cream to the freezer container, cover and freeze until set. Transfer the ice cream to the refrigerator 30 minutes before serving, to soften slightly.
4 Heat all the ingredients for the chocolate sauce, if making, gently in a saucepan, stirring until melted. Serve with scoops of the ice cream.

For chocolate double mint ice cream, make the ice cream as above, adding 2 tablespoons chopped fresh mint and 20 g (¾ oz) crushed peppermint sweets to the whipped cream and milk. Freeze as above, then stir in the melted dark chocolate mix.

chocolate & pistachio soufflés

serves 6
prep + cook time 30 minutes

butter, for greasing
25 g (1 oz) pistachio nuts, ground
150 g (5 oz) plain dark chocolate
    (72 per cent cocoa solids),
    broken into small pieces
4 eggs, separated
100 g (3½ oz) caster sugar
2 teaspoons cornflour
cocoa powder or icing sugar, for
    dusting (optional)

1 Grease 6 x 175 ml (6 fl oz) ramekins, then lightly dust with
1 tablespoon of the ground pistachios to cover the base and sides.
(This helps the soufflés to rise.) Place on a baking sheet.
2 Melt the chocolate in a heatproof bowl set over a saucepan of
gently simmering water, then leave to cool slightly.
3 Meanwhile, whisk the egg whites in a clean large bowl with a hand-
held electric whisk until stiff, then gradually whisk in half the sugar until
the mixture is thick and glossy.
4 Stir the remaining sugar, egg yolks and cornflour into the cooled
chocolate mixture. Gently fold some of the egg white mixture into the
chocolate mixture, then gently fold in the remainder, with the remaining
pistachios. Spoon into the prepared dishes and spread the tops level,
then clean the edges with a fingertip.
5 Place in a preheated oven, 190°C (375°F), Gas Mark 5, for 20 minutes
or until risen. Dust with cocoa or icing sugar, if using. Serve immediately.

cinnamon-spiced cherries

serves 4
prep + cook time 10 minutes

25 g (1 oz) caster sugar
350 ml (12 fl oz) rosé wine
strip of pared lemon rind
1 cinnamon stick
500 g (1 lb) cherries, pitted if liked

1 Combine all the ingredients in a saucepan. Bring to the boil, then reduce the heat and simmer for 5 minutes until the sugar has dissolved and the cherries are tender.
2 Use a slotted spoon to transfer the cherries to a serving dish, then cook the liquid over a high heat for 3–4 minutes until syrupy. Remove the cinnamon and lemon rind, then pour over the cherries and serve warm or cold.

Tip
Fragrant with cinnamon, this quick and easy dessert is delicious served over vanilla ice cream or with a dollop of Greek yogurt on top.

baked figs with honey & pistachios

serves 4
prep + cook time 20 minutes

12 figs
25 g (1 oz) butter, plus extra for
   greasing
2 tablespoons soft light brown sugar
2 tablespoons runny honey
3 tablespoons orange juice
½ teaspoon ground cinnamon
25 g (1 oz) shelled unsalted
   pistachio nuts

1 Lightly grease a small, shallow roasting tin. Cut a cross down into the top of each fig, then arrange them in the tin. Place a little butter on each, then pour over the sugar, honey, orange juice and cinnamon.
2 Place in a preheated oven, 200°C (400°F), Gas Mark 6, for 12 minutes, then scatter over the pistachios and return to the oven for a further 3 minutes until the figs are tender. Serve with natural yogurt.

roasted pears with oriental spices

serves 4
prep + cook time 45 minutes

4 pears
8 tablespoons dry or sweet sherry
8 tablespoons water
6–8 pieces star anise
1 cinnamon stick, broken into
  pieces
8 cloves
8 cardamom pods, crushed
50 g (2 oz) unsalted butter
4 tablespoons light muscovado
  sugar
1 orange

1 Leave the peel on the pears and cut them in half, down through the stems to the base. Scoop out the core, then put in a roasting tin with the cut sides up. Spoon the sherry into the core cavity of each pear and the measured water into the base of the tin. Sprinkle the spices over the pears, including the cardamom pods and their black seeds. Dot with the butter, then sprinkle with the sugar.
2 Remove the rind from the orange and sprinkle into the tin. Cut the orange into wedges and squeeze the juice over the pears. Add the wedges to the base of the roasting tin.
3 Cook in a preheated oven, 180°C (350°F), Gas Mark 4, for 25 minutes until tender and just beginning to brown, spooning the pan juices over the pears halfway through cooking and again at the end.
4 Spoon into shallow dishes, drizzle with the pan juices and serve with crème fraîche or Greek yogurt.

heavenly chocolate puddings

serves 4
prep + cook time 20 minutes

100 g (3½ oz) milk chocolate,
   broken up
50 g (2 oz) unsalted butter
40 g (1½ oz) cocoa powder
75 g (3 oz) golden caster sugar
2 eggs, separated
1 teaspoon vanilla extract
4 tablespoons single cream
icing sugar, for dusting

1 Melt the chocolate and butter in a large mixing bowl placed over a pan of barely simmering water, making sure the surface of the water does not touch the bowl. Remove from the heat, add the cocoa powder, 50 g (2 oz) of the sugar, the egg yolks, vanilla extract and cream and beat the mixture to a smooth paste.

2 Whisk the egg whites in a clean bowl until peaking and gradually whisk in the remaining sugar. Use a large metal spoon to fold a quarter of the meringue into the chocolate mixture to lighten it, then fold in the remainder.

3 Spoon the mixture into 4 small ramekin dishes or similar-sized ovenproof dishes. Bake in a preheated oven, 160°C (325°F), Gas Mark 3, for 8–10 minutes or until a very thin crust has formed over the surface. Dust with icing sugar and serve immediately.

For boozy chocolate puddings, stir 2 tablespoons brandy, rum or orange liqueur into the mixture with the cream. Continue as above.

orange & rosemary polenta cake

serves 6–8
prep + cook time 30 minutes

175 g (6 oz) unsalted butter,
   softened
175 g (6 oz) caster sugar
finely grated rind and juice of
   1 orange
150 g (5 oz) ground almonds
2 large eggs
75 g (3 oz) coarse polenta
½ teaspoon gluten-free baking
   powder

for the orange syrup
grated rind and juice of
   1 large orange
50 g (2 oz) caster sugar
2 tablespoons water
1 tablespoon chopped rosemary

1 Line a 20 cm (8 inch) round cake tin with nonstick baking paper. Place the butter, sugar and orange rind in a large bowl and beat with a hand-held electric whisk until light and fluffy. Add the ground almonds and eggs and beat well. Stir in the orange juice, polenta and baking powder and mix until well combined.
2 Spoon the mixture into the prepared cake tin and place in a preheated oven, 180°C (350°F), Gas Mark 4, for 20–25 minutes until risen and firm to the touch.
3 Meanwhile, place all the syrup ingredients in a saucepan and bring to the boil. Reduce the heat and simmer for 2–3 minutes.
4 Spoon the syrup over the cake in the tin, then turn out and serve in slices.

Tip
Polenta, another name for cornmeal, is naturally gluten-free, so is useful for cakes and desserts.

cherry & cinnamon zabaglione

serves 4
prep + cook time 25 minutes

4 egg yolks
125 g (4 oz) caster sugar
150 ml (¼ pint) cream sherry
large pinch of ground cinnamon,
    plus extra to decorate
400 g (13 oz) can black cherries in
    syrup

1 Pour 5 cm (2 inches) water into a medium saucepan and bring to the boil. Set a large heatproof bowl over the pan, making sure that the water does not touch the base of the bowl. Reduce the heat so that the water is simmering, then add the egg yolks, sugar, sherry and cinnamon to the bowl. Whisk for 5–8 minutes or until very thick and foamy and the custard leaves a trail when the whisk is lifted above the mixture.

2 Drain off some of the cherry syrup and then tip the cherries and just a little of the syrup into a small saucepan. Warm through, then spoon into 4 glasses. Pour the warm zabaglione over the top and serve dusted with cinnamon and with amaretti biscuits.

marsala poached pears

serves 6
prep + cook time 50 minutes

300 ml (½ pint) Marsala
500 ml (17 fl oz) red wine
200 g (7 oz) caster sugar
2 tablespoons lemon juice
1 cinnamon stick
2 star anise
6 pears

1 Put the Marsala, red wine, sugar, lemon juice, the cinnamon stick and star anise in a heavy-based saucepan and bring to a low simmer.
2 Peel the pears, leaving the stalks in place, put them in the saucepan and cook for 20—25 minutes, turning occasionally, until they are soft. Remove the pears from the saucepan with a slotted spoon and set aside to cool.
3 Meanwhile, return the poaching liquor to the heat and boil to reduce for about 10 minutes until it is thick and syrupy. Serve the pears, drizzled with the syrup and accompanied by a spoonful of clotted cream.

Tip
Available both sweet and dry, Marsala is a fortified wine from Sicily. Use it to enhance gravies, sauces, desserts and risottos.

creamy lemon & almond rice pudding

serves 4
prep + cook time 30 minutes

100 g (3½ oz) short-grain pudding
   rice, rinsed
50 g (2 oz) caster sugar
grated rind and juice of 2 unwaxed
   lemons, plus extra rind to
   decorate
100 g (3½ oz) sultanas
450 ml (¾ pint) boiling water
410 g (13 oz) can evaporated milk
25 g (1 oz) flaked almonds

1 Place the rice, sugar, lemon rind and juice, sultanas and measured water in a saucepan and simmer, uncovered, for 20–25 minutes. Stir in the evaporated milk and simmer for a further 5 minutes until the rice is tender.
2 Meanwhile, place the almonds in a hot frying pan and dry-fry for 1–2 minutes until toasted.
3 Pour the rice pudding into serving dishes and sprinkle with the flaked almonds and extra lemon rind. Serve immediately.

Tip
Evaporated milk is fresh milk with 60 per cent of the water removed. It is not the same as condensed milk, which is very sweet.